44

Expectation Days

Elegies for the Hot Season
Radiation
The Year of Our Birth
Sensing
Patron Happiness
Pheasant Flower
Responsibility for Blue
Floralia
Streamers
The God of Indeterminacy
Beauty in Use
Edge Effect: Trails and Portrayals
The Spaces between Birds:
    Mother/Daughter Poems, 1967–1995
A Visit to Civilization

Expectation Days

Poems by
Sandra McPherson

University of Illinois Press
Urbana and Chicago

Library of Congress Cataloging-in-Publication Data
McPherson, Sandra.
Expectation days : poems / by Sandra McPherson.
p.   cm.
ISBN-13 978-0-252-03234-9 (cloth : acid-free paper)
ISBN-10 0-252-03234-9 (cloth : acid-free paper)
ISBN-13 978-0-252-07475-2 (pbk. : acid-free paper)
ISBN-10 0-252-07475-0 (pbk. : acid-free paper)
I. Title.
PS3563.A326E97   2007
813'.54—dc22   2007011383

Acknowledgments

Grateful acknowledgment is made to the following publications in which some of the poems in this volume first appeared, several in slightly different forms or with different titles.

Agni 63: "The Bat by Porch Light." "Poem for a Late Birthday," (originally titled "Poem for My Fifty-first Birthday)," *Field: Contemporary Poetry and Poetics,* issue 52, spring 1995, 69; "Blossom River Drive" and "Children of the Village" (issue 64, spring 2001, 18–19, published by Oberlin College Press, © Oberlin College). *Grand Street:* "Hibakusha." "Virtue Study: Pastoral" first published in *Harvard Review. Missouri Review:* "Surfaces, Central Valley, 190°." *Poetry:* "On Being Transparent" (September 2002, vol. 180, no. 6); "To a Book of Needles, 1918" (October/November 1997, vol. 171, no. 1); "Grouse" and "On Suicide Watch" (March 2006, vol. 187, no. 6); "Virtue Study: 'It was his first'" (October/November 2002, vol. 181, no. 1). "Beach Journal, May: Dune Census" reprinted from *Shenandoah: The Washington and Lee Review,* with the permission of the Editor. "Gospel Disinclined" was first published in the *Kenyon Review*—New Series, Summer 2004, vol. 26, no. 3. "Two Young Trees Bending in Strong Wind" was first published in the *New Republic.* "Officer and Gentleman and a Small Heroic Order" was first published in the *Paris Review* 170 (summer 2004); "Precipice, Rush, Sheath" was first published in the *Paris Review* 120 (fall 1991). *Yale Review:* "Chicory at Night"; "Autumn on a Small Tree"; "Pre-Op Room"; "'Through Lace Curtains, Ravens' (Pasternak)"; "Virtue Study: Samma Vaca." "How to Read an Aerial Map" first appeared in *Lighthouse Poems,* a handprinted limited edition published by Thornwillow Press in 1999. "The Mexican Acrobat," "Muses for Panic," "Bereavement: 1919," and "Diary: Day of Rest" first appeared in *TriQuarterly. Western Humanities Review:* "Fox." *ZYZZYVA:* "Cabawaguni Scarecrow"; "Expectation Days"; "Do-It-Yourselfer's Ghazal."

Epigraphs: (1) From *The Wild Braid: A Poet Reflects on a Century in the Garden* by Stanley Kunitz and Genine Lentine. Copyright © 2005 by Stan-

for Susan Kelly-DeWitt,
Virginia Whitney Weigand,
and Pamela Moore Schneider

There are areas where you want the garden
to suggest the variability of the emotional life.
Too many gardens I've seen seem to express only one mood or one
state of being. There is a dependence, a reliance
on the effectiveness, let's say, of a single color,
as though it were the only state of being that corresponds
with one's concept of the beautiful.

—Stanley Kunitz, *The Wild Braid*

And as one single body did not suffice for so long a time,
it was necessary to proceed by stages
with so many bodies as would render my knowledge
complete; this I repeated twice
in order to discover the differences.

—Leonardo DaVinci, *Notebooks*

Contents

III

IV

V

I

Grouse

This water flows dark red
from alder tannin:
boot-stain river

between white rocks.
An ouzel, flannel-feathered,
sips the current up.

Mossgatherers
spread their patches
across a dry, flat turnaround.

They seem embarrassed,
want to shelter in the dark.
A coyote running in broad day;

stumps ruffling
with sulphur polypores
woodsy to the tongue,

woody to teeth. Early
yellow leaves paste river to its bed;
blackberries drop, the last,

many out of taste
and strictly smudge.
Puddles loop in the road:

Bottomland—
the foolhen
waits there for

the fool gun,
gray throat-down free in a burst,
the pose, the afterslump.

Carcass beside spirit.
O come to my hand, unkillable;
whatever continues, continue to approach.

Beach Journal, May: Dune Census

"Is distance necessary? If you said yes,
You no longer live where you grew up . . ."

Or so I dreamed, adding that the furlongs
Of early explorers fulfilled a need, wet and scratchy

Distance on a horse,
Turbid nautical miles.

I had been poisoned, disjunct from amicable mind,
The body I crouched in and pummeled with rough wishes

Profaned by medicine, hands secularized in work,
The wind in my pine-cool eyes checked

Without meadow light
Or sea glare.

When I survived, I leaned to the window
In time to see blue plumage fly

Down into the sea-fig's cresset.
I was in the real world: hundreds of shoreline shrines

Low to the ground or airborne in an osprey's hooks,
Quail parishes, sand churches, holy shrubs, furtive godsons of fog.

There were farnesses of dune grass
Woven by wind into mounds, acres

Of baskets rolling right up to the house,
Their lading salt-air.

"Is distance necessary?
If you said no, you're a snuggler,"

Health, wanting to stay, claimed sleepily.
I went out: in the bank of the bleached sand road

Broken armor of a crustacean age; earthenware chips
Between manzanita roots;

Miner's lettuce,
Its sake cups

Moored to leaf's center by ruddled, bronzed umbilicals;
Blue-eyed grass tapped by poppy in a ditch.

Questioned from outside the sky,
Who answers well? White strawberry vibrates slightly

In a force that convulses trees;
I barely stand higher

Than cow parsnip, tall as a calf;
I stew over minor pimpernel, look into

The painted peal of a foxglove bell. Maybe I'm quizzing it.
And I, so far away, can hardly hear that bell

Until I take up the lens . . .

"Through Lace Curtains, Ravens" (Pasternak)

"Sunshine" and "Summer in Norway,"
the childhood piano sheet music,
the roaming ghosts of family pets,
a geranium rug, a bear-brown pelt-pile couch.

And, in the kitchen, spilled sunburn
of southern-exposed tomatoes, frank leukocytes
of cucumbers. Off linoleum burnish,
a refrain of feeding those spectral cats.

Then, discreet almost Quaker alcohol
eked out into nearly invisible jiggers
to toast the family elders in their graves
across the window's river in the rose-barbed hills.

Something in the woman practicing
ideal fingering of songs
remains her age at her first birth-giving.
The man washing dishes, though, feels he

always counted, before even the flutter
of a first son. At sunset there are other rooms
the phantom darlings find,
a cellar where scheming cartons

store maternity smocks, baby-smelling toys,
up against the rain-sopped, fern-rooted
foundation, in case
the couple's aging daughter—

whose husband has made
even everyday deliberations difficult
by going mad, his mind, all he knows
as *self,* a lace curtain

through which a powerful raven
seems entangled,
mosaicked, netted, snowflaked, a stenciled crow—
chooses motherhood.

Gospel Disinclined

The baritones and tenors simply will not sing.
My Wurlitzer's mistakes of hand sound very loud.
Their heads lean either down (but are not bowed)
or back (but not in ecstasy of gaze upon the Lord).
The sky's rise wavers dusk before the evening food.
(Something about that semi-light distracts:
Is it rays off lemons blunted, mulled? Ascent
of walnut smoke? Dried duffels of purple grapes?
Seedpods rattling on a catalpa tree? Sky candlelight?)
Now won't their senses sing to them? The mission
heavens lighten one degree with corner lamps.
Someplace—a ceilinged sermon—to faint into, to live
cut out for. Is each man a solo, solitary? Or surrounded
by a season's end of the sloppiest best-of-friends?
Who'll dare to mouth a hymn? Forgive—
my favorite key's D ♫ flat. By devotion
of a sexton the garden sleeping grounds
pacify, embraced by vines and trees.
Earth, our deluxe van, keeps its route around the sun.
Urine runs. One brother dawns or pales. I play
by ear for all the stumbling voices still to hear.

I Was Young and Working
by the Ship Locks

The boats used to float upward to us.
Skippers who, I knew, had not fallen from cliffs
rose from their sinking
to the base of what was now our precipice.

Once, I went *through* the locks.
The boats were afraid to touch each other.
Captains yelled across their decks and up their masts,
then fell quiet, tense and forbearing in the lay-by:

Our portly red fenders scrape
     coarse concrete walls, scratch silken algae
arras. We drop as low as we can,
     then overwhelming gates open to the sea.

Back at evening, we stalled our hull
at the foot of the clenched chamber;
the whole wide Sound tapered
to this compass point between mole and breakwater.

I thought
our crew would never be as light
as the gates' eyebrows, never lift
as easily as cynic foreheads raise.

The doors were not rococo. If anything,
they were stubborner than the dead
Messiah's stone and they intended
to box Him in.

Eventually they gave
every moody voyager permission to ride
up and be freed, airy and lightsome, to the lake.
No more narrowings.

Yet I need more. I want locks on the stairs
  and out in the street,
 at a door to an obedient office.
   Latching. Transferring me there

where I cannot, by my own
  floating progress, my own ark-like cheer
 and sporty flag, and salvatory nature,
   advance, face those draining places.

Officer and Gentleman and a
Small Heroic Order

Watching a re-run of the movie favorite
Where a dejected naval would-be hero
Hangs himself in a unit of the aquamarine
Motel (right over the starfish and tide),
I recognized where I spent my first marriage's
Wedding night (I'm sure the groom thought
The moon, if not his pregnant honey, looked fine),
Where we awoke to an unwakable battery
In the just-bought old used Bug.
                                            The re-run
Oppressed me for a day or two
Until I remembered how I saw them filming
One of the scenes, a martial arts match
In the hangar. The star wandered among our crowd
And told us nicely to be quiet soon—
Oh, happily—and it took so long,
Waxed repetitious reshooting the takes
Because you can't count on every nicety
Working no matter how ardently
    Everyone tries.
                              What we see on screen
Is not the way it feels to make a thing,
And even with the suicide,
Probably, I don't know, they just had to keep
Trying. Probably the movie's joyous outcome
Had to be undertaken many times
In case the players weren't happy enough
At rightly-lit moments, in the gradations
Of apparent emotions and real weather.

I know the climate, am used to its drizzle
(Tormenting to some). But when it opens up
You can see all the way out of your own country
And into a completely different dominion,
Vast Canada, as if there actually may be
A boundary strip of astounding clarity out there,
Blowing around above whitecaps or paddling
To stay afloat.
                    And sometimes a real
Winged periphery forms
By orange-billed word-of-mouth, by rank
Still called wild, a fine-cut file of puffins,
Uniform, polished, as if they were trained
To dive and disciplined to drift.

Precipice, Rush, Sheath

(on a cliff at Yachats, central Oregon coast)

"Hold, just grab the grass," counseled my link
to the humanized, floricultured top,
when—on the incoming tide, the waves
tall and brown in a fog, basaltic
black sand submerging rough under foam—
we decided to leave by the cliff, take the face
up through roots, wrap each grip
around a tuft.
              I did clutch one
and identified it then as "Juncus
Lesuerii," a rush, not a grass,
clove-colored rumpled corsage on whose stalk
we depended. There, a stark, care-cut,
unforeseen inflorescence burst and froze
while midday darkened, sky pulling in
the heavy blue of mussel shells.

Beneath the overhang, only this thatch
kept our midway, unbelonging bodies
from falling through its garden
without footholds. It held only hands.
And we had to turn back, without turning around,
greet in reverse all the salt
rush which would lower us through
the plant's world-view
of the descending sun.

Imagine: this edge, the wind blows,
and you nod here, energetic and cellular,
in your green sheath after dark . . .

Two Young Trees Bending in Strong Wind

Vehement curtsies—
as if they compulsively
respect each other.

They bend to the same south
but toss heads differently.
Overeager, one shakes.
Courtly, the other nods.

On their recoil, sparrows dissect
the trees' airspace.
It is not kowtowing. It is twisting,

a motion to help the light
on half of each
reach most of each.

No one has given them a stake,
whalebone,
jib.

In an idiosyncrasy of wind,
I have seen them bow
towards each other

against the cloud-dark paint
of a subdivision wall.
Storm-beings,

young confusions
of bad weather and good manners,
they are mature like us already—

polite, driven.

On Being Transparent: Cedar Rapids Airport

(October, 2001)

If they raise a picture
Of three ingots afloat, or suspended
In discrete shadow-prone directions,
    And do not know
What I am carrying between
The soap's diminished oblong
    And the underslip's commercial lace,
If they do not recognize these sandbars aiming through
The small and doleful stones in soles,
    It is my duty to guide their hands
By voice down into baggage of their doubt,
Carry-on of risk, make common
    The roots
(Inside the hunting ducks) of lead
That held them stable in the streaming lakes
    Or swaying upright in the homely slough.
No battle, just ballast. Then I nod respect
To soldiers at their jobs,
    To genders in identical camouflage,
And to the searchers far far younger
Than the bachelor scaup and widgeon couple
    I am bearing home. Of personalities—
The winning, the horrific—
There really isn't any mortal scrutiny
    Trained enough to sort
Transcendence from the gross ungodly.
I want such a machine.

And a machine will suffice: A god
Is too boundless for mere citizens' safety,
Too unwieldy for my preemie-diaphanous-hair's-breadth
        Mysticism—uninspected
But true-to-soul: the one-time visitation
I cling to of a presence glowing . . . like a
        Golden mayfly.
It came aboard my nerves, lodged
In a reading-light-sized chamber
        Over my left eye,
Where it could radiate unquestionable security,
Peace, and rest. I still carry the gift
        Of its short but sacred flight.

Lucid Dreaming: Oxycodone

WDP 1955–2002

If his hallucinations had a season,
They were spring's. The pear dispelled
   Small opal movie screens,
On each an animation, gracile, clowning.
   They courted me—and yet
I found them hard to audit,
   Answer, nod agreement with.
Of the ways I could say, "You're dreaming,"
   I learned to choose a voice
Of pleasured caring. For both
   Of us, the dream pronouncement
Verified he had an "inner life," a nucleus of marvel
   That he feared forsook him
In the lull of a waking interval.
   I couldn't picture his unknown
Or covert void—he was so brimming
   He overflowed to feel any vacant space.
Where was that core of a confidential cloister
   With its pelargoniums around a well,
Tiled cisterns and reflecting pool
   —that date-palmed peristyle
He'd wrapped with saints, singers, trumpets,
   A splendid inner life?
Wrecked, uncultivated, what?
   And so when he whispered
I should buy medallions for dressing up dogs
   Or revealed the "I'm a little grandpa" secret
Or pointed to five men he noticed
   "Counting a green fish"
Or introduced me to the Concertina Brothers
   Or asked how many people I saw

Put on feather suits in our living room,
     Coaxed me with
"Let's go shopping for mirrors in the dark,"
     That was his newfledged
Lucidity. I stocked my blues
   ─ With midget fish I thought he'd like.
Though with no hope of growth, they saw
     Through big clear eyes. "We'll fall in love
With trains again," he said one time
     To lift away the chronic pain.

II

Containers

Keep nothing in them.
But avail yourself of them.
Trace the ether of their diameter.
No lid—
says air
astir.

Basic
basin.
Space
place.
Room's home.
Praised with
patina.

I've emptied it of summer berries
and filled it with wooden fish—
American copper basket:
tooled until figured with shadows;
surfaced with the tempo
to cart, to bear.
Bumps and wood-grain and petal-wrinkles.
Did I
"have to be"
made?

Sarít collects vessels.
Some smell of incense,
some grew from trees

and some from metals
heated to their cores and outward
to our rooms.
You know what a shout
does to them?
Nothing that hurts.

The husband's urn: room for pet
and wife
to mix
in time with him.
"The best urn ever."
He would have said so,
firefighter
in life, in reliquary
for the glow he quenched.

Bowl wisdom: To desire is good
as long as not to
desire is good.

How bowls grow:
by hollowing.

A fissure : clamp.
A split : rejoin with brass.
Householders needn't make another bowl—
Tuareg (Khadija, Mebarka, Zohra) decorate the wound,
rig it with bangles of staples.

To *endure the world's wear*—
The privilege—

Nwando said
It might take a month
of practice everyday
for us to learn
how to carry water
on our heads.
A jar
with all it already knows
laughs down
at a mind
that doesn't know.
I may be
a water-portrait
on the ground—
but the jar
is the tall jar
it is.

Receptivity,
continuous depth to edge—

Then there's
a ladle,
life in a ladle,
lifted
by one small
handled bowl
up over the greater bowl.

Living with an Urn

Not the urn, but the vase is clear.
The vase lives with the urn.

I can set up a spot breeze
wherever a guest needs fanning—
a portable source of ease.

Through lace panels to the south,
plum leaves twist like shiners.
Chairs without visitors
hold cats or manuscripts.

It's not perfect
order when you have to tell people
what they're sitting with in the room—

easier to point out a merganser
or an eagle-beaked man of Himalayan wood

or an anthology whose cover you could wear as a mask,
than an urn on the grand—like an aquarium
riding on a shark.

I play "Always"
only once in a while.

Bereavement: Leaving the Radio on
All Night for Company

8 a.m., waking,
Johann Sebastian and Doc

on my sheeted chest, after which
they play Strauss

and I am bitter about mere godless dance
until I grip

my unsexed, so-loved boy
in place and sway and sigh

and he purrs, if that is music,
prone, if that is dance,

me leading and humming until I sing
as he closes his eyes and nuzzles in pleasure

to the waltzes from the south . . .

Bereavement: 1919

Believing I am going to live,
I begin the war of nerves.
When I need just a little calmative
I drink top milk at the creamery.
But toward evening let me recommend
This, should you ever need it—
I hang a locket of asafetida around my neck.
Works wonders.

Pre-Op Room

Not much festooning: a wall like a syphoned mural,
A close-out vision, plumb, janitorial
Semi-glossed cleanliness. In its foreground,
      I am a life form.

—What is your favorite color?
—Smeared *mamey,* red-apricot, the fruit of paint.
Or *tlapalli,* Rivera's Náhautl deep
      Reddish purple brown.

—What is your favorite stone?
—Basalt. Lava tubes. Black sand.
—Basalt ring and pomegranate gown, then,
      Nurse Lavender says.

Murmur Navajo: Journey in beauty
On your gurney. Intend to stay conscious.
Not beauty-conscious. Nurse Dhallie tends
      The flicker of pale zeal

Burning on nothing in my fasted mind.
Where's its old luster? Tripping as instructed:
Tracking down paths that are part of me,
      Their twill fern-weaves,

Sempervirons' summits and their squirrels,
Boulder-pebbles down a draw: a garden,
Surely, made to line the chasm
      Of this melancholy.

Nurse makes me reconvene these charms.
A drawstring bag that stores
My thoughts' belongings. I will not empty out
        Unless I say *Complete.*

And I do remember whole, healthed,
Consummated life, equally as well
As Cavafy held, inscribed, such
        Uncompleted longing for it.

Muses for Panic

I

On the recommendation of my body
a black sun appears in the clouds,

solar breathing stops, our carriage
tosses without hearth or bowl or bed.

The expanse is all blind gray, my heart
a greasy knob. Monochromatic,

the airspace bars all stars.
The others and I are pent.

I have my seat-mate's pulse in my wrist.
Stellar's jay clamor

comes hoarse from my ears,
my panting's say-so.

My feet snap,
hands flood,

my eyes move like the worm
split by the spade.

We will come low, fracture
bells and teapots, pool

with the ichor
of chickens and dogs,

rubble the beachside dance pavilion.
Watch for me in your

closets, muffs and gloves.
Flab, release soul. Soul, sign me

and feather the dust off—
that will be your trust.

2

He probes,
standing straight down on a leg bone,

pressing there
for an evolutionary measure of time

before he accepts it and curls—
the way we test out a stone

that might wobble or flinch
in a creek we're crossing,

before we accept that we *are* crossing
because we need the other side.

Then he will coil
tight against me, so that my body says

not to move. Defer to fur.
I have felt his tennis-ball head

just fit my hand,
his sporty skull create dragonflies

to carry in his mouth so carefully
he can play with their *burr*ing

desperation. I coddle
the brain that smells mice

in the fragrant rosemary
and thinks to rub a bat over my books.

Timidity sometimes backs him
into a mound of quilts till nothing's showing

but his eyes like pennies in the lint trap.
He'll leave me lonely in a thunderstorm.

How could his father forsake us
for the other side?

3

The physician is late:
This ploy is to discompose the mind

a body usually leans on.
To my thrown fit

he fits his beacon hose.
I try to recognize my own turns

and twists. I learn new ones and I speak
as if I'm the guide.

I want to lead.
There is a She in there,

just as much esteem
as the Who in the mirror.

Further the tardy oppressor asks. That is
my goal too. Push ahead with the lamp.

Till it hurts so much I'm
histrionic: eyes cry out when stage-light

unmasks, unveils
what should unman him,

the heroine's
shy unknown.

Suicidology

1

Those who watch,
Those who watch praying—

The cursing one,
The curled and pillowed one—

"Pointless" (why say that?)—
"Think of myself too much" (and not kill the thought)—

Now the late voice of a true friend from a book—
Then the tiny speech of Issa, a bug in slippers—

Now out watering the jasmine lizards—
Hands ruffle the feverish flat geranium petals—

What color? Tango. What other color?
Crucifixion parfait.

Yes, he is reviving, stirring back—
The care pamphlets settle below the directories.

2

Glad cat teethes on the doorknob.
Cycle or salvage the yellow

Legal pad contract "Not to"?
That year, caretaking, I saved him—

Left the page in his right to tear out of age.
Took ring with goldsmith's sunrise off his left.

How adept at dawning, those extinct
Starting places, the clay doorway into a timeline,

Gourd seeds planted
To grow water jars—

Farthest cheers,
He'd cached enough for one:

His hard drink,
Plain tap to fool me.

3

When we living feel our dead's hand—
That's how we glean we are both.

I hold his fingers, slightly blanched
Flat butter beans, once climbers.

Stones in the rock-yard
Breathe more through ore of their grit

Than does his back—
His pose comes to a stop. He'd wanted a pen

With nib and ink, he liked nicety,
Had patience with a holding pattern, fancied script

From the future heirloom.
Diagnose it: It isn't poet's cramp—

He numbed
His touch

From the heart out:
They mail me, officially, all I can know—

Autopsyturvy.

Mourning, Ninth Month

If I am altering,
trying to intercept my inner targets
with some shift in aim,
lighting the bales with the old moon's shell
neither meaningful nor purposeful
just looking well,
                I'll change
with some obedience, wishing I could recognize
the force. I don't know yet if it is thoughtless.
Many beautiful formations on earth
are made without hope, but with winds and rivers
in its stead.
              Is my national park
a widow, carved then saved, and a draw
for visitors
whose pity erodes to awe?

Post-Op, Medical Humanities

Compared to my husband's kiss
during a camera's long violation
of the nautilus
membranes of my inner Cinerama,

this procedure is brief
and the nurse has studied haiku.
The surgeon's
written children's books,

so read me to sleep, make believe
to numb me. The society of my big toe
scrawls and hews and will mend,
but with no kiss to spellbind.

In eight weeks, though, the M.D.
surprises me with a hug.
We schedule my second healing
arthrodesis at the dancing axis

of a leg. Again I feel love:
it's for a hurt fish foot in a net,
scaly and violet and gill gold,
a fetish of his memory.

Wife of the perished,
snugged by sutures,
in dreams and under anesthesia,
I offer my arch to caress, extend the original

kiss back to his ghost's dazed pain.
Beyond medicine, he passes me
his opus-in-draft
of the poem of heaven

trailing like loosed dressings
until I can stand,
as knit and as alone,
as his last last line.

Fox: A Memory of My Husband

(after an observation by Gerald Durrell)

The breath of a fox
May wait a million years
To rain on the oak
That heard the animal pant.

The oak will not be there;
Or not that one—
Some patience the oak left.
I am the she-fox

Remaining to respire
And sigh
The sparse cloud, the strewn mist
That is you.

Now is the reviving snow of New Year,
When I call the dishonest furnace repair
And carry lengths of Carlos's
Downed apricot tree

In to be burned. A sizzle
From the breath of the fox.
3, 4, 5 a.m., bark-shine and smoke,
Your alder-speckled back

Not here.
But the torrid woodstove works,
And in the morning the mottled
Serviceperson reeks of oil,

Fingerprints the furnace, doors, his chin,
Takes my first money of the year
And edges out
Where frosted lilac leaves

Splay flat and do not wag.
I dab
White ginger essence on a dried lei,
Wish for your cress-scented cheek,

Its breath delaying
In snowflake, glacier, sea.
In cumulus pushing rain.
It will come back to me.

Or not to me . . .

III

Cabawaguni Scarecrow, Dang Region, Nepal

The lower castes were called upon to chip out the statues, the bridge guardians, spirits straddling fountains, and the sacrosanct scarecrows. They made these powers out of wood, found that a face is best chopped, not whittled. A blunt look, protective. And menial hands. I count all the fingers in prayer and carve them upward, righteous hedge shears. I have the rounding body of one who has never outed a figure from wood. Bodies like ours should grow wool. Be a Himalayan sheep, an *abrash* of a brown animal, an old lady ovine, lanolin-thighed wide trail-crowder. The sky is full of crows' brains twice a day; like morning and evening newspapers, they talk to dazzle and frazzle the page. Please don't shoot them. They add up to much intelligence. Communal body—we drink milk, trough water, bug juice. We should bounce this happy flock flesh. At night, on the corner, in the cold of a distant month, a *frostitute,* lowly and a thing of dreams, forms as language crystallizes in my waking. Taut jewel that won't melt when hot. One sequin that all the crows' eyes can spot.

Do-It-Yourselfer's Ghazal

The friends drilled and clattered the frame together, threw their tools among poppies burgeoning between the pathway's river stones. Roof and walls lay side by side. Cooperation felt like trying. Blood drops surrounded the shed. Enough trying! Nearby, plump roses won over a hard part of the garden. A bird-sown palm orphaned up behind a rock. Each of us decided to keep making an effort. "One would have to have seen boathouses to know if those are boathouses in the picture," Sol said. That stopped me for a while—the seeing of boathouses, not a right of experience, not in every regional cosmology. "Can you say you have seen a boathouse?" I describe the moans and clanks, the queasy rising and tilting, the shouldering to the side. The mystery of trees aswim. Huge beams backfloating. Once I saw a bear swimming, during the tension of a marriage. It was offshore quite a distance. It knew where the island was. The bear swam to that island. I waited until I witnessed that.

Expectation Days

Memorial Day weekend, Arch got a WWII Red Cross nurse tattooed on his twenty-year-old forearm. Very nice. I went to my stash of armbands and workers' kerchiefs, gauzes, dittybags, and helmet liners with Bible verses penned on them from Vietnam. I thought he'd like to see old blood along with the cute nurse. Massacred tattoos of every war colorize the memorial battlefields the way, as Whalen says, the ink of poems barely holds old Chinese paper together. Because no wishes came from my flesh and blood, I bought myself a Mother's Day gift, a bear with M•O•M stitched on its paunch, which is better than the drafts of "21 love poems and a song of despair" crinkled on my own. Doc's rough tongue keeps his hair alphabetized. The paint-mixing man at Wal-Mart used the word "miracly" today, refreshing, by concentrating, the time of amazement as he pushed many samples of black-eyed loud yellow around and around.

Blossom River Drive

My childhood friend sent me his novel forty years later, the street with the gentle, sickly boy, with traffic of caterpillars (that no longer drop in), with Pete the unseen indoor sot, with garden cloche front windows, with an assortment of ordinary neighbors who put to use the decorations of each season to become one lyrical whole. Fish ponds and filled-in ex-ponds, the twine and rigging of willow glades, hazel thickets, rose plots, and the evergreened back of an old farm mansion from whose land the rest of ours was carved. That garage with its combusting rags. Canadian first names, Mexican surnames, Italian singers, Greek restaurateurs. Pass the schoolyard now and I see transparent silhouettes at play. An air of dolls and ropes and balls. The gowns of brides begin toy-size. Bantam grooms. Narrative rabbits and wolves as familiars. Capes and eye patches, petite, prophetic. That is how we toyed with the mature, the grown. We were complete; only later did we winnow, forget, pretend not. The doll's grandchild is someone's daughter the mechanic. The novelist's father died, bereaving the book, practically a grandson. Now we are caught up, aren't we? A long-running trouble for beauty sustained us, or the beautiful would not be visible for us to see involuntarily today. Or to catch by ear: in first words, as they attune to this present.

Children of the Village

(in memory of Isaiah Shoales)

His short life had been one long boy's thought, and now they were illustrating it with pictures. At the funeral his condition was painted by bold preaching: "Death is a moving van." A snowy dove perched in an ivory cage beside the boy. Its eyes turned here or there, for hour after hour of prayer. Probably it was not overcome by the choir singing in the way we were awed, mornings, by the oratory of wings. The part-Siamese heeded my torch song as he lingered on the sill to watch a breeze. He understood the verse's "weather"; he understood the rhyming "feather." Phoebe's blown glass piano at last had been unpacked from its memoried box. Demise of her ardor for pianos, so I inherit miniature grands from my own child. Ardor—if you look at the instrument in its dusty casket, you see it is frosted with tracery of a fragile too-high-to-hear Diabelli variation. For actual music, we have pines. For remembrance, scent of mandarin blossoms in the dark. What kind of a childhood is it for one diagnosed as a stranger? When Ruma brings over her cello for the trios, the child lingers and listens. She plays with the sound of sticks under the crabapple the woodchucks frequent. Some worn ivories of an upright are her first. A perching bird intrudes, flies through and up into the ceiling, up the stairs, so high that the parents are amazed and fretful. Soon after that, this child began to reason out the Baroque, which she played like an understanding, an accord between her favorite diagram in Gray's Anatomy and a milkweed pod as it bursts.

Schoolchildren, 2000 and 1848

In custody, the boy thinks: *I'll be beetle*
scrimshaw, folk art of worm-wended bone,
and my testosterone still be extolled
as silencer of my English teacher.

A schoolgirl, same calendar age,
plied her cheeky poetry, as pious
as it was ghoulishly true, into linen
rose path and blossoming hedge.

Dangers stand thick through all the ground
To push us to the tomb,
And fierce diseases wait around
To hurry mortals home.

While silkwork finches fetch grass
for a tea-bowl nest, her needle
needs no apology as does a gun.
Buds and berries balance the germ.

She signs, *Ann Williamson.*
Undwindled red, her Plymouth flowers
look as peppery today; and darkling verse
inches straight ahead.

Her schoolmistress provisioned her
with all she'd need to know
for her memorial sampler, prophetic
for Barry Grunow.

Note: Barry Grunow taught English at Lake Worth Middle School in Lake Worth,
Florida, from August 1993 until May 26, 2000, when he was shot and killed by
Nathaniel Brazill, age 14.

The Mexican Acrobat

I stood on top of the linen cupboard where neither my cat nor I had stepped
before. I promised him his turn if he could just wait, with supportive eyes,
till after I'd hung the Mexican acrobat right under the cathedral ceiling.
The acrobat has a way of boosting us high even when the painting rests on
the bed. Over the little Mexican village storm clouds saturate with color
paradoxes. The acrobat waves atop a pole on a man's head. Right outside, I
found a crow feather to lift up a mantis with. Green aglow on black aflame.
I "flew" her to the apex of a prickly rose. She was threatened
>   with play
>   by a paw.
Then paws raced October leaves down the middle of the street. A person
in the morning love poetry class is going to see a young death. She says she
doesn't want to miss any class. She likes the discussion, and the laughing. A
tree burning from a Nazi V-1 resembles a person with the bark peeling off,
wrote the painter Godderis. It is a farm outside Antwerp, where he took
his paints and his family to feel safe. A bomb burns up seasons, which, as
appointed as they are, nonetheless begin to look like freedom. Trumpet and
drum: in *el campo,* to balance above the palm trees is one way to serve up
a circus to the angry clouds.

IV

Virtue Study: "It was his first"

It was his first
Gingerly little chain-
Sawing, a ring too tight,
Which had been on
Since eighty-two,

The year he was born.
"It grows," he showed me,
"Like a tree," the finger
Around the constriction.
"Yes," I said, "look how much

You grew in eighteen years.
No wonder I can't
Twist it free." His eyes
Worked nervously,
Yet, his hands calm, it fell

Open in three seconds.
Just takes a spinning
Wheel in a crescent
To cut through
Shackles of gold.

This, I know, will
Be encouraging for him.
He'll remember it
Tonight. He'll be able
To refer to it

For the rest of his memory,
As a first, succinct and civil, his role
As the sunspot that nipped the glare,
A severance attained
With perfect sympathy.

Virtue Study: Pastoral

The famous prose writer,
with his morel woods and bass pond

and charming one-room schoolhouse,
grabbed his horse syringe

and led the poet's girl away to the barn.
They small-talked of her medical bent—she adored

syringes. (Her mother'd seen her
watch with elation

in the children's clinic, each inoculation
in her own upper arm.)

And under the gaze
of big horse eyes against the hay,

spectators as grand as red oaks
that pull down lightning,

she listened as he implored through ripples
of her flat t-shirt

to come in to meet the sister forms
smaller than fermented crabapples

the besotting woodchuck guzzles,
and, more, to kiss them.

Since this was not the first grown man
to solicit, the child pronounced

no, she was just interested in the way
to minister to horses,

to help them heal, burgeon,
to make them better, even in a manner

she thought the horses might sense
is best.
        Often in writing workshops,

in every group of people
looking after each other,

the needful compare
confessions, their cold-case shock,

in poems resembling this draft.
What would we do with this version—

change "adored" or "prose"?
Or try to hear the girl relay it once

out loud, then, for herself, snip up
short pages, fetters re-wrought

as the chain of a wordless paper novel
about the famous prose writer and his morals.

Virtue Study: Samma Vaca

Deer reflected on salamanders, black-quilled wind-flower,
trail, boats, log lodge, all
gone under the heels of the roar.

The loneliness of my regret
says *don't speak* and *right speech.*

Right noise, eating pine nuts, quiet fish.

An echo needn't puzzle over well-speaking.
It has no accountability.

It imagines, though, the facility to mutter.

In the low waterlands of valley ponds,
a bit of grammar:
otter slide prints, hare claw divots.

Underneath all architecture is an unconstructed spot.
Off the face of the earth:

deep, dark, chill Spirit Lake . . . nonexisting . . .
trying all the harder to say the right thing.

Virtue Study: Teachings

"I took my care and doubt after your spirituality seminar
to a church where I learned to get closer to God at every moment.
Every Tuesday, every Thursday, for the summer months,
I fasted to be open to God. He lives in me always.
I thought the fasting would be hard—
but it was a piece of cake."

Nicole's email in 2000. She said my aura is emerald.

Xavier Martinez's hand-painted postcard, 1920s:

"Only the primitive's prayers work."

The woad blue West, yet did not sell at auction.

From a catalogue raisonné:

"As if the artist, in a sudden panic, was forced to admit,
'My God, I've no idea how to paint at all!'
This primitivism . . . certifies the artistic conscience
at work, ever seeking to renew itself."

Student to teacher, artist to apprentice, devotee
applauding painter of the tawny East:
all, at their moment, empty, fasting, and feasting on conscience.

Note: The third quote is by Brian O'Doherty, p. 132 of *The Figurative Fifties*, as
    documented in *Fairfield Porter: A Catalogue Raisonné of Paintings, Watercolors, and
    Pastels*, New York: Hudson Hills Press, 2001, p. 225.

Virtue Study: Happy Hour

Once, reading of blossoms and
besottedness of great
haiku poets, I accepted
their empty sake
casks, good

for bringing my own lavender and yarrow in—
for they admired rice, approved moon,
boated and fanned,
and never spoiled spring
nights with anything—

apart from words trying to ferment.
Their images patched
the rent silk of stomach,
liver, head. No mother's milk
was ever sipped

from such light syllables,
nor falling on the stairs
unscrolled
in such transportive verse.
My idols'

gazes rolled
up like pear blossoms
in March, tolled round
and round like hail in April.
They did write it pretty

once, those poets
before car keys.

Virtue Study: Blues Society

(WDP 1955–2002)

In the audience pressed dim,
e pluribus unum,
at the foot of a quintet
staging live renditions
of Percy Mayfield's sadness
and Willie Dixon's power,
of heartache and backbone,
a woman raises her partner
with a single smooth ascent—
not a jarring or winching,
not a shaky wobble.
(I was going to ask Walter
for weight-training words
before he rose
irrevocably sick of heart,
from our address of earth.)
The woman's gift to her friend
is an elevating from the wheelchair
(a movable transcended tomb):
She slides her up, emplaces her
where she can steady
that benumbed body
against her own and lean
into the drowsy dance,
her hands spread wide
in a disposition of nerve—
like roots over granite
on a lake island.
The two are on their own
shore of the dance floor,
closer to the lappings than I.

To the still woman's mouth,
wrested to the side,
her complement dabs
a candid white-on-white
handwork handkerchief,
reworks her webbing palms
into a fishnet bolster
(and if there were
a raising to life,
my husband would weigh nothing
in my blue arms' sway)
as if lifting a saved drowner
from the water and over
the side of the boat to music.

V

Chicory at Night

This far from civilization,
what station could be coming in?
Five caravanners brazen in their lamp;
two of us drifting off inside a tent.

Pardoning myself, I call
to the nightlifers and their teenage daughters
dancing at midnight through the fishing camp.
Will they blow out their noisy candle?

The cliffs char soft as outer stones
of a dying cookfire; the river, black
as run-off from a blaze,
has settled below plateaus it nurses;

now it's backwater for a dam. In sleep—
were it here—I'd receive friends
quietly in tune, who never think they are
the only people in a landscape

stoic as this, a crewcut desert,
channel marker pegging the John Day's
astringent, swaying passage
to a butte's reflection. Nothing paddles across.

Tonight the current's blank as Conelrad's.
At its edge, boats massage the dock,
a mild thistle turns white with age,
and a pink-cupped, stripe-hipped primrose

inhales shut these hours the neighbors
broadcast, Colonel Someone and his cousins
from Rufus. Our tent's framed open,
I try to listen to its own strange music

breathe through the six flutes
of the frame-poles; to hear my first husband,
still Private when he left the army,
clang his marching trombone in the trash,

retire it to mouthless music,
to listening without a fight.
Today we ran the boat below the dam
milling and pulling underhull

island-length paisleys, a shawl
of a current, tinted with minced fish
from the turbines. The paisleys came at us,
all holes and swirls, dam spittle, swells

of phosphorescence sieving through them.
We fished in the eddy's slick green patio plates—
until the army engineers changed the current,
raised a new pattern of quilted floodgates, opened

a lock. The tower of a tug entered white,
grew grayer, then black as the sleep
we can't catch up with tonight. Gulls
turn the biggest wheels. I don't know

which world this is, the uncivilized or
the powerful rudeness of civilization.
The mantle of a big gas lantern
casts the officer's loud shadow-bust

across the tent, a colossus thin
as brain cells on a slide.
Just retired; no more "Yes, sir";
now he's playing Dixieland.

Through bluffs of sleeping chukars,
rattlers, kingbirds, killdeer,
water-lap and spider-step, I pester:
Stop, some people are trying to sleep;

to invite neighbors awake demands a friendliness.
Beneath the surface, the current
makes no sound against itself,
rimrock's muttered all over with cow trails,

the silence echoes for more peace.
"It looks as if everyone's asleep,"
relations shooting the breezeless night
with the officer remark and squeal

with laughter. This rivermouth enters the side
of another river. Fifes, I think,
the tentpoles are fifes beneath this black locust,
cornerpost of the Colonists,

stabilizing their homes in the wilderness.
And I give up begging, slipper out
beside the chicory looking at night
as if its flowers had been cut,

making itself look this way,
snapped at the stem-ends
as if it chewed itself to sleep.
As if the loud people in camp

talked its head off. But if
at night it appears clawed, picked, blue
coffee one has to bite, it yawns open mornings
all sky spokes, deep-dyed filaments, growing

out of the ruts beside RV's.
Waste places. Books for civilians
on the wild say a woman watched for a sailor
until she tired and closed her eyes,

but in the morning her eyes blued
with him. And this is why
she was turned into chicory,
into this sailor-flower I watch in the sand?

Goodbye, green soldier.
Out of uniform, this flower is just me
turning and turning
things over in my mind,

a woman revolved to look like a victim
to silence her attacker.
The chicory tweaks and mangles its fringes.
But in the morning it will open half as dusty

as a flower that stayed awake all night.
It will seem like more
than any man's war
can kill on sight.

Diary: Day of Rest

The poplar tops buck, inflate, die down,
and shake to a stillness, righted, not wilted,
magnolia petals brushed out on the lawn.

On the radio a man would give his life
for inspiration, shouts belief in Saint Paul's rules.
And missionaries shoulder to shoulder at the door
ring a bell to tell me God is not a racist anymore.

Quick, fold your cards away, our parents had said,
the youth pastor's coming.

But now: I feel breathed in,
the body worked to a suppleness at last, its age
more than ever welcoming fresh scents.

The opened daphne fanned inside—
into my ears, around in hollows under my eyes.

March 13. Mirrors reflect a storm
top to bottom, wind chimes echo
its pearly pandemonium.
Same date last century: We'd be smart women
who did all Sunday work on Saturday,
saying it was ordained.
Then no one holier or heavier could force
chores from us on our day of rest.

It's Sunday so no grown daughter can expect
the letter her mother never writes,
its bulletin of nervous aspirations.

I believe: no credence ever,
ever,
without curiosity.

A divinity's apt to be busy today—
scanning rest,
from all exposures reverencing
the apple-blossom atom.

To a Book of Needles, 1918

In *our time,* respecting
the making of seams, gathering and ruffling,
there is no combat for a woman with needles.
She may even abstain from the thimble.

But *once upon a time,* running toward the seamstress
with their bayonets, out of the gilt illumination
of bombardment,

the doughboys on the OVER THE TRENCHES brand
inspired seven different gold-eyed weapons,
bodkin- (for elastic), darning-, wool-, yarn-,

cotton-, carpet-, and button-needles,
driving her through the Great War, the gentlewoman crossing
her legs on the back panel of the needle book.

Her eyes are smiling
at the end of the thread
and the oval aperture seeing through the Iron Age

that will draw together all her pattern pieces.
However fair and adorning, each work must be spurred
by the torn boys on the front.

Italians have the sense of beauty. Everywhere the soldiers
made wonderful little gardens
flanked by sea shells in front of their dugouts.

In these, flowers were growing.
The shelling
was never sea shells (are they *fire* and *husk* in Italian too?).

The infantry and their gardens
open as opposites, like the folded
volatile front and peaceable back
of the needle book.

Featherweight thread fighting in your peewee armor,
in *our* time we need to unfold the packet,
view the diptych from the same side,

see the mind that had to suture these two cultures
in sharp advance.
Finished into one: maker, the liberators

armed to unmake,
and the creation at hand,
held until whole, from scratch.

Note: Material in italics is modified from Harry Emerson Fosdick's article in the
Independent, Nov. 9, 1918.

The Bat by Porch Light

Night, when I was flying across
the sleep of other lives,
your pet reached out and snagged me
from the balcony, in the web of my cape . . .

This gore lays itself out for your lionheart,
who feels less companionless
nosing over the mousy
bird of me.

I feel, just behind the right shoulder, clean teeth
become my own spare bones,
a synchronous skeleton.

We live together briefly, the tom whispering
in my ear, me tolling
a squeal.

But the arrest weighs on me.
Night's old neatness mussed. Here I am
indoors, bleeding all over the house-
mistress's books, everything I knew forever
jounced from place, my slant on things

flattening to the floor. A kind neighbor
drowns me. Phoenix sloshing in a pail.
He drops me on a glacier.

I await the county man
who picks up iced identities.
Death is my address
on the flyway to South America.
And my sound—

like hair after hair uniting on a cat's back—
migrates among the rabid searchers,
who will find out
I was well.
As is, therefore, your treasured
mugger.

Hibakusha

"They can marry each *other*," he says.
The car is cool, white leather.
"They can marry each other."

Streets of palm, fields of fennel,
Hills of pink oil tanks.
We pass faultline and mothball fleet.

They can't marry each other, I say,
If they love someone younger,
Who isn't a survivor, who's too young

To have survived. They must marry
Each other, these survivors, though no one
Wants them for fathers, for mothers.

A vineyard, a river, an acre of sheepskins.
My father has driven all this way
To save me the trouble.
He, my daughter, and I commute

Past windmills on blanched hillsides.
Fresh blades. Oldest of energies
Lathering new wind.

And they don't marry each other,
The contaminated, the irradiant.

I think they are looking for lovers,
Going round and round in the wind,
Looking for lovers.

Poem for a Late Birthday

The boat has been upside down for
the last five blooms
of hydrangeas that harbor it.

The boat is a stranger's boat,
stranger's hydrangea.

The boat does not grow
but it grows as its slivers
pull apart, pull discrete
as if for better view of one another.

The purpose of the boat
is now out of the hands
of navigators.
Fish

no longer see its shadow.
Oar? Motor?—
just the savor

of the grass,
and a tendency to drift.

Some ship!
Shallow as it is,
isn't there still draft to deepen in?

Out from under the bow
a cat—

who knows
how long it had been cagey, watching?—
a cat comes into the open,

high tail, one candle.

How to Read an Aerial Map

War Department Field Manual, August 1944

"Shadows must fall toward you."
And they have, with the approaching faint
of the staggerer, with the wail of the broken hipped,
with a childlike trust in my direction.
Shadows must fall toward me
and I accept their imposition,
I am composed, I am there for them.

Now the shadows are old and the forests stripped.
War used to be lit like this, rough glow
telling on every surface. Duty chose,
between white road and meadow-threading path,
a watertower boiling on the burner of its shadow,
a camouflaged warehouse named by its truthful shade.

Do I know where the maps went?—
they were torn into blurs, burned
into clouds and beams, buried in bits.
Did the courage that held them
ever ask to be paid in light?
Gossamer, cameras, and tears
have more of that than governments.

If it happens again, I have strength
for one or two more downfallen shapes.
The first one I learned on, clear and dark;
the proof, if I search, is still in my arms.

On Suicide Watch

Will the little figures ever reach the monument?
A doctor orders me to be on watch.
    Will the mist pass over their cheeks
    and clear the strollers' eyes?
If so, I'll see it. I'm on watch.
I train my eyes on paintings
to see if there is any change.

My patient draws
a blank on landscapes on his walls.
    What did Daubigny observe that pastel afternoon
    that made him want to live?
    What did Fairfield Porter want to stretch
across the sky, blue pennant of a family park?
Watcher, stop—you've been thinking of artists with some fame;
look to the person wiping out his name.

In time the impasse
    of the monitored one's mouth
changes from pale sky
to a kindling of light above the trees.
    Unmoving water-studies stir.
    "Look *now.* It will never be more fascinating,"
Schuyler said and I do.

    But I couldn't always see,
and I can't see him at all anymore.
    He lived through this vigilance a year.
On occasion, in the mirror, I recognize
    the ghost of my old post,
a dim print of my assigned design,
while keeping myself, my meaning
    something to live for, in full view.

Autumn on a Small Tree

After shyness,
I grew to offer almost anything in public.
But that valor—

abashment will track it down; I've wanted
razors for some meant
display of awe. And spontaneity

earns reconsiderations,
pooling of reflections
talented to drown.

I don't know if the tree,
its fifth autumn,
still tenses with surprise.

Or becomes kinder
—that sometimes saves one—
befriends the imperceptive air.

But there is no more privacy finally.
The tree tries the first yellows it thinks of,
then revises, revises, in front of all.

I think I've seen it let
the leaves it hasn't grown yet
fall first.

Surfaces, Central Valley, 109°

The electric fan revamps old air over old, lasting quilts, yellow and white, against dark wood, a lenient, murmuring condolence. Long summer brightness eats down through dark leaves. Hedges veil farms. Porcelain, old print, ancient picture frame profit this shop a dollar. After their useful life, the objects have insomnia until some soul returns their gaze and makes them the picture of use again, decorated for their service at the ceremony of their purchase.

Down the side street the cheaper, more "flea,"
more anthropological shop's framed O.
J. Simpson in a Hertz ad.
Antiquities everywhere . . .

Here in the apollonian, peaceable, cottage-roomed emporium called Bon Marché the shopkeeper polishes a crowded quietness. No dust, no apparent worm at work. A reupholstered hush becalms completed lives. The ottoman says with rested regard, "One life, it's done, the rest is honorarium." With voice in reserve, "A little something."

A plate's
a plate to go home with you. Cup by cup
cups leave the rooms. None means
to remain this time next year.

At the produce stand, there's sulfur in the well. Backyard obliges hanging grapes and crawling squash. A forgotten onion from another year blossoms up through strawberries against a fence. Inside our home the glass on all the paintings turns to window screens. The hat-racked, full length mirror mimics a screen door. The creek. The latch. The threshold. Look out to oleanders spilling onto shoulders of subliminal country roads. The pines are cracking, crackling at their tops. Pine nuts small and black snap off, fling out. They line the ditches. I walk—it feels like creek-fording—to a neighbor's to get a trout.

Distant big-city radio: "Super Equis."
When we choose
music in tongues other than our own
the mood is clearer. We do not pretend

we know the words for how we feel.
Burning pine nuts and dented objects
say things we feel too.
A shimmer becomes

one more screen
over the screens.
One more degree and there are
no surfaces.

SANDRA MCPHERSON is a professor of English at the University of California, Davis. She has also taught at the University of Iowa Writers' Workshop, the Oregon Writers Workshop, and the University of California, Berkeley. She has won a Guggenheim fellowship and received an award in literature from the American Academy and Institute of Arts and Letters.

Illinois Poetry Series

Laurence Lieberman, Editor

Healing Song for the Inner Ear
Michael S. Harper (1984)

The Passion of the Right-Angled Man
T. R. Hummer (1984)

Dear John, Dear Coltrane
Michael S. Harper (1985)

Poems from the Sangamon
John Knoepfle (1985)

In It
Stephen Berg (1986)

The Ghosts of Who We Were
Phyllis Thompson (1986)

Moon in a Mason Jar
Robert Wrigley (1986)

Lower-Class Heresy
T. R. Hummer (1987)

Poems: New and Selected
Frederick Morgan (1987)

Furnace Harbor: A Rhapsody of the
North Country
Philip D. Church (1988)

Bad Girl, with Hawk
Nance Van Winckel (1988)

Blue Tango
Michael Van Walleghen (1989)

Eden
Dennis Schmitz (1989)

Waiting for Poppa at the Smithtown
Diner
Peter Serchuk (1990)

Great Blue
Brendan Galvin (1990)

What My Father Believed
Robert Wrigley (1991)

Something Grazes Our Hair
S. J. Marks (1991)

Walking the Blind Dog
G. E. Murray (1992)

The Sawdust War
Jim Barnes (1992)

The God of Indeterminacy
Sandra McPherson (1993)

Off-Season at the Edge of the World
Debora Greger (1994)

Counting the Black Angels
Len Roberts (1994)

Oblivion
Stephen Berg (1995)

To Us, All Flowers Are Roses
Lorna Goodison (1995)

Honorable Amendments
Michael S. Harper (1995)

Points of Departure
Miller Williams (1995)

Dance Script with Electric Ballerina
Alice Fulton (reissue, 1996)

To the Bone: New and Selected Poems
Sydney Lea (1996)

Floating on Solitude
Dave Smith (3-volume reissue, 1996)

Bruised Paradise
Kevin Stein (1996)

Walt Whitman Bathing
David Wagoner (1996)

Rough Cut
Thomas Swiss (1997)

Paris
Jim Barnes (1997)

The Ways We Touch
Miller Williams (1997)

The Rooster Mask
Henry Hart (1998)

The Trouble-Making Finch
Len Roberts (1998)

Grazing
Ira Sadoff (1998)

Turn Thanks
Lorna Goodison (1999)

Traveling Light:
Collected and New Poems
David Wagoner (1999)

Some Jazz a While:
Collected Poems
Miller Williams (1999)

The Iron City
John Bensko (2000)

Songlines in Michaeltree: New and
Collected Poems
Michael S. Harper (2000)

Pursuit of a Wound
Sydney Lea (2000)

The Pebble: Old and New Poems
Mairi MacInnes (2000)

Chance Ransom
Kevin Stein (2000)

House of Poured-Out Waters
Jane Mead (2001)

The Silent Singer: New and Selected
Poems
Len Roberts (2001)

The Salt Hour
J. P. White (2001)

Guide to the Blue Tongue
Virgil Suárez (2002)

The House of Song
David Wagoner (2002)

X =
Stephen Berg (2002)

Arts of a Cold Sun
G. E. Murray (2003)

Barter
Ira Sadoff (2003)

The Hollow Log Lounge
R. T. Smith (2003)

In the Black Window: New and
Selected Poems
Michael Van Walleghen (2004)

A Deed to the Light
Jeanne Murray Walker (2004)

Controlling the Silver
Lorna Goodison (2005)

Good Morning and Good Night
David Wagoner (2005)

American Ghost Roses
Kevin Stein (2005)

Battles and Lullabies
Richard Michelson (2005)

Visiting Picasso
Jim Barnes (2006)

The Disappearing Trick
Len Roberts (2006)

Sleeping with the Moon
Colleen J. McElroy (2007)

Expectation Days
Sandra McPherson (2007)

National Poetry Series

Eroding Witness
Nathaniel Mackey (1985)
Selected by Michael S. Harper

Palladium
Alice Fulton (1986)
Selected by Mark Strand

Cities in Motion
Sylvia Moss (1987)
Selected by Derek Walcott

The Hand of God and a Few
Bright Flowers
William Olsen (1988)
Selected by David Wagoner

The Great Bird of Love
Paul Zimmer (1989)
Selected by William Stafford

Stubborn
Roland Flint (1990)
Selected by Dave Smith

The Surface
Laura Mullen (1991)
Selected by C. K. Williams

The Dig
Lynn Emanuel (1992)
Selected by Gerald Stern

My Alexandria
Mark Doty (1993)
Selected by Philip Levine

The High Road to Taos
Martin Edmunds (1994)
Selected by Donald Hall

Theater of Animals
Samn Stockwell (1995)
Selected by Louise Glück

The Broken World
Marcus Cafagña (1996)
Selected by Yusef Komunyakaa

Nine Skies
A. V. Christie (1997)
Selected by Sandra McPherson

Lost Wax
Heather Ramsdell (1998)
Selected by James Tate

So Often the Pitcher Goes to Water
until It Breaks
Rigoberto González (1999)
Selected by Ai

Renunciation
Corey Marks (2000)
Selected by Philip Levine

Manderley
Rebecca Wolff (2001)
Selected by Robert Pinsky

Theory of Devolution
David Groff (2002)
Selected by Mark Doty

Rhythm and Booze
Julie Kane (2003)
Selected by Maxine Kumin

Shiva's Drum
Stephen Cramer (2004)
Selected by Grace Schulman

The Welcome
David Friedman (2005)
Selected by Stephen Dunn

Michelangelo's Seizure
Steve Gehrke (2006)
Selected by T. R. Hummer

Other Poetry Volumes

Local Men and *Domains*
James Whitehead (1987)

Her Soul beneath the Bone: Women's
Poetry on Breast Cancer
Edited by Leatrice Lifshitz (1988)

Days from a Dream Almanac
Dennis Tedlock (1990)

Working Classics: Poems on
Industrial Life
*Edited by Peter Oresick and
Nicholas Coles* (1990)

Hummers, Knucklers, and Slow Curves:
Contemporary Baseball Poems
Edited by Don Johnson (1991)

The Double Reckoning of
Christopher Columbus
Barbara Helfgott Hyett (1992)

Selected Poems
Jean Garrigue (1992)

New and Selected Poems, 1962–92
Laurence Lieberman (1993)

The Dig and *Hotel Fiesta*
Lynn Emanuel (1994)

For a Living: The Poetry of Work
Edited by Nicholas Coles and Peter Oresick
(1995)

The Tracks We Leave: Poems on
Endangered Wildlife of North America
Barbara Helfgott Hyett (1996)

Peasants Wake for Fellini's *Casanova*
and Other Poems
*Andrea Zanzotto; edited and translated by
John P. Welle and Ruth Feldman; drawings
by Federico Fellini and Augusto Murer*
(1997)

Moon in a Mason Jar and *What My
Father Believed*
Robert Wrigley (1997)

The Wild Card: Selected Poems, Early
and Late
*Karl Shapiro; edited by Stanley Kunitz
and David Ignatow* (1998)

Turtle, Swan and *Bethlehem in Broad
Daylight*
Mark Doty (2000)

Illinois Voices: An Anthology of
Twentieth-Century Poetry
Edited by Kevin Stein and G. E. Murray
(2001)

On a Wing of the Sun
Jim Barnes (3-volume reissue, 2001)

Poems
*William Carlos Williams; introduction by
Virginia M. Wright-Peterson* (2002)

Creole Echoes: The Francophone Poetry
of Nineteenth-Century Louisiana
*Translated by Norman R. Shapiro;
introduction and notes by M. Lynn Weiss*
(2003)

Poetry from *Sojourner:*
A Feminist Anthology
*Edited by Ruth Lepson with
Lynne Yamaguchi; introduction by
Mary Loeffelholz* (2004)

Asian American Poetry:
The Next Generation
*Edited by Victoria M. Chang;
foreword by Marilyn Chin* (2004)

Papermill: Poems, 1927–35
*Joseph Kalar; edited and with an
Introduction by Ted Genoways* (2005)

The University of Illinois Press
is a founding member of the
Association of American University Presses.

_____

Composed in 11/14 Adobe Garamond
by Jim Proefrock
at the University of Illinois Press
Designed by Dennis Roberts
Manufactured by Thomson-Shore, Inc.

University of Illinois Press
1325 South Oak Street
Champaign, IL 61820-6903
www.press.uillinois.edu